ONLINE DATING

IT CAN HAPPEN TO **ANYBODY**

REMY HETRICK

outskirtspress
DENVER, COLORADO

Outskirts Press, Inc.
http://www.outskirtspress.com

ISBN: 978-1-4787-5498-5

Contents

About Online Dating:
My True Story
It Can Happen to Anyone

CHAPTER 1

Warning Signs, Do's and Don'ts

IN THE BEGINNING, I wasn't sure I should tell the story of what happened to me. I was afraid that I would be embarrassed, or that people would judge and reject me if they found out how stupid I had been in not figuring out sooner that I was being duped. But I was vulnerable and lonely, and I made a mistake. I didn't figure out that I was talking to an impostor, and I kept talking to him, thinking that maybe finally I had found the man of my dreams. There are many times in our lives, we don't want people to know of what is really bothering us. Not even to those people who are closer to us. Not even to our own children. Because you are afraid thinking of what their reaction would it be once they will find out. Then one day I start telling few people because I want to let out of the guilt that I am feeling. I thought they will understand and will give support and better judgement about what happen, instead they told me some kind of criticism by telling me that I made a bad choice. That I should know better. How could I not think?....After hearing these painful comment, the more I felt down and felt sorry to myself. I was very disappointed I immediately having more fear. I realized what those people are saying is only an opinion which is the exercise of human will but it sure don't help me anything. I became very negative. The more I do not want anybody to know....I isolate myself away from people. If I am talking to someone I cut it short and pretend like their was nothing wrong with me. I try to smile but deep inside is a big lump of bitterness and heartache. I am not good in pretending. That time, keeping it quite is the best way to do even if it bothers me. For awhile I am in a denial. I don't want to talk about it for fear of getting embarrassed. I also try not to think about it....but it always come back specially when I am alone. I am as miserable as it can be. I admit I made a mistake. This is the reason why I start telling people. Instead of me feeling better by doing this, the more it affect me emotionally. No one understand??... Before all of these happen, I was a person that never quit. I am always positive. I always find solutions to my problem no matter how big it is. I don't let my mind focus on negative things. In other words, I don't throw myself into that kind of predicament for a long period of time. I always have a positive idea in making the right decision. I don't know why this time... it seems like I cannot get out of it. Before this incident happens, in many occasions I been approached by people who happens to have problems and they will tell me about what is bothering them. I guess they don't have anywhere to go and no one to turn to who can help them like me. I love helping people. It makes me happy to see that I can put smile back to their face even just by talking to them and telling them that their is HOPE and solutions to their problems, instead of making them more frustrated and helpless. Who am I to judge and make them feel worst. I want to help if I can even when sometimes I am Frank and straight forward in expressing my inner thoughts but I try not to offend people in anyway. I don't make things worst of the difficulties they already facing in. Now I understand how those people feel. I am in the same situation as they are. This time I wondered why I cannot apply the same concept to myself. Why can't I not face my own adversity? My mind is like a roller coaster. I didn't join online dating looking for trouble. I am looking for love and companionship. This whole situation makes me felt like I am in a desert that no one is around but me. No one understand what I went through. So I cried day and night. If I fall asleep, I woke up in the middle of the night crying so I get up and pray. Going to bed and falling asleep is hard to do. Once I'm in bed I will remember everything. I don't want to be alone because the more I will think what happen. The whole situation change my personality as well. All my life I loved music but this time I hate listening to it. I know the devil is playing a big role of what is happening to me. He wanted to destroy me by playing and manipulating through my emotions. I know if I won't do something I will be in a brink of depression. We are always under attack everyday of our lives. Satans goal is to paralyzed us with fear and torment us with negative emotions. The way I feel just like sitting in a rocking chair. I won't go nowhere instead it's draining my energy every single day. I am wasting my time in thinking about it. There is no other choice but hand it to God. For He is in control and I cannot rely with my instinct. He can change me little by little. I know He hasn't give up on me. So this time I had to pray more. I talked to God our Lord Jesus Christ more often than before. I bend down my knees and pray many times a day so He will give me wisdom to make the right decision. I talked to God so He will direct me to the right path of how I am able to do and to where I suppose to go. I pray that God will give me a stable mind in dealing with my problems. And I cannot do this on my own without His Help and Mercy. After all the Bible says, "THERE IS NOTHING IMPOSSIBLE" to those who believe. I believe that I might not get the sun but He will give me the moon. Who am I is my gift to God. Who I will become is His gift to me. By doing this it made me enlighten. I was thinking some people do stupid things when they have problems. Some of them rely on drugs, some drown themselves with alcohol while others even commit a suicide. I do not want these things to happen to me. I can't imagine the feelings...One day while I was driving to work , I felt like I want to turn my radio on in my car. So I did. As I turned it on, the station was playing Gospel songs. One of the songs that was played is by Marvin Gaye, " HIS EYES ARE ON THE SPARROW". As I listen to it I start crying again. But this time I cried because I'd realized that I am wasting my time in worrying the things that it already happen and I cannot do a thing to bring it back. I made up my mind. After all nobody will help me but me. I have to help myself. I was thinking that God answer my prayers by making me listen to the song. I ask myself why would I let those negative people and this negative feelings bother me. I don't have to mope around and feel sorry to myself anymore. Regardless of what happen I can't bring anything back. I realized those people never been to this kind of situation that is the reason why they don't understand. I cannot make people change nor I cannot make people agree with me. I have to make my own changes and apply the right kind of attitude in dealing with my own problems in order for me to get out of it. One thing I was worried is my health. I was so stressed out that I cannot sleep. Stressed can lead to so many health issues. I been in this situation too long. It's my life .... After all, this not about them. This is about me. I cannot let those people or fear destroy of who I am, what I am in the eyes of God. By knowing God, there's nowhere you can go or do that God is not. He has a unique one of a kind plan for me. So many things that happen in life is a test. And I am not anyway different from others. I am a human being who made mistakes. I am very special no matter what those people think. I believe this happen for a reason....Here I am from that time on, most people I talk to they are the ones who encouraged me to write and tell my story. This time I found people not only understand my situation but also very supportive in my decision. It took me at least a year and a half to put my life back together even if I already begin writing this book. Every now and then I still remember. My experience made a drastic impact in my life I hope that this is not the only way that I can do to stop those criminals from victimizing those vulnerable people to get money from the Internet. They are not only taking advantage of the system but they are also using the word "LOVE" to do their dirty work. I have to let go of my fears and tell my story. I want people to have the opportunity to learn from my mistakes, and I hope to help others to avoid being taken advantage of. My story involves international issues, but that doesn't mean anything; this could happen with someone right here in the United States...the person lying to you could even be your neighbor. Lying online

is very common on dating sites. You've probably heard a lot of stories about online dating.
Some stories have a happy ending, while others are sad. My story is unique, because it is
both happy and sad.

I got inspired to write my story after I started telling people what had happened to me.
My co-workers who were listening to me said
I should write about my experience and pub-
lish a book. They said they wanted to know
what really happened. So I decided to tell my
story in detail. I want my story to serve as an
example to men and women, young and old,
who use online dating to find their soulmate. I
hope readers will learn something from me. I
am not saying that all people are bad, and I'm
not trying to discourage people from using online dating. I just want to alert people that they
should be careful and aware, because people
who misuse online dating sites are very good
liars. Some people are lucky and find love online—but then there are the others like me,
who are not so lucky.

Online dating is a great option for people

who don't have time to go out, or people who are tired of going out. People from all walks of life have success stories about using dating sites. It's more convenient for a lot of us to go online to meet the person of our dreams. I wish my story were as happy as some I've heard, but instead, I had the opposite experience. Be aware when you start talking to someone on-line. Don't rush into things. Hold your feelings back, and investigate. Ask as many questions as you want. When you start a conversation with someone, be sure you know the details of what they are telling you. Limit your trust, es-pecially if they are in a foreign country. Don't take what the person says at face value. Make sure that he or she wants to meet you as soon as possible. If it's been a month or more and you still haven't met, that's not a good sign. In some instances it may take longer to arrange a meeting, and you must use your own judg-ment, but if this happens, ask why the person can't make time to see you. Don't assume—find out the facts.

If you are talking to someone online and

you have already developed deep feelings for this person, and it has been a month or more since you started communicating and you have not yet met him or her, then forget about them. Stop talking to this person. More than likely, he or she is just fooling around, and has no interest in meeting you. Don't make yourself unavailable to the other members. I know sometimes it's hard to let go of someone, especially if we are attracted to the person and our thoughts and feelings are telling us this is the one. But there's a better way to handle it; if there are a few people who want to talk to you, give them a chance. Don't settle for one person immediately. Explore. The main reason for this is that if the person doesn't work out, you still have other people to communicate with, and you are giving yourself the opportunity to know other members. It means you'll have a back-up.

The other reason not to limit yourself to one member is to protect against a scam. Don't be a victim like me. Find someone else who is willing to meet you, because if you settle for someone who doesn't want to meet you, more than likely the picture you saw is of someone who doesn't exist. Usually that kind of person will create lots of excuses not to meet you, even if they've said that they will. Their common excuses are that they are working on a project deadline, or they are too busy at work, or they're having a family problem, etc. But the truth is they don't really have any intention of meeting you, though they will keep you on the hook by making promises. Probably they don't want to meet because they are using someone else's picture, which they've stolen to post on the internet.

If you choose to communicate even if you haven't met the person, be ready. Invite him or her to talk on a video chat, such as Skype or FaceTime, or any platform that lets you see him or her closely. Let the person stand up while taking to you, and be sure that you can see the person's face. If he or she won't agree to do this, then stop. This is the mistake I made. I didn't invite him to talk to me using video chat. I only thought about the man's picture, and I was infatuated with his good looks. I was crazy not to do video chat with him when I had the chance. One way of knowing that this people are fake is when you ask them to write on something and wave their hands while they are in the video cam. If they refuse means the webcam that you are looking at, is a fake video which they create.They knew and they are prepared for this to happen. Remember lots of scammers are very good in creating things since many of them are well educated. If you are a man beware of a picture that look like "Sport Illustrated Magazine Model" This is a red flag. Some of these con artist will give you their bank account and password so you can get into their fake bank account for you to see as if they have lots of money in exchange to your bank account number. They will tell you to transfer some of their money to your account. This is one of their many tricks that they do. Some of them will talk about inheritance that they will inherit but the bank is holding the money because they have some kind of issue about it.In other words they wanted you to help them by sending money to them. Or they might sent you a large amount of check so you can deposit it to your bank account. If this will happen make it sure that you tell your bank to hold the check and verify before they will deposit it to your account to avoid any kind of problem ones the check will bounce because it is fake.They will do this in exchange to your money. Some of them they will tell you that they have problem about their mortgage. Or they will tell you that they will send something to you but the custom is holding it since their is a fee to release it. Don't buy on this because these are scam. It is typical for a scammer to professed their feelings first and they will tell you that everything are fine. Eventually problems will arise. Once you get hooked that is when they will talk about problems of any kind to get money from you. They wanted you to help them by sending them money. They will use this as an excuse so you feel sorry and have compassion for them. They will do their trick by telling you what kind of problem they have. There are thousands of stories that this people create just to get money from you. One of them is SEX. They will used sex as a tool to get you to fall for them. Be aware!!! Once you start sending them money, they will tell you to send it so different places like France for example or India, maybe Los Angeles because they also have connections to these places so it won't look like money laundering. Remember they are in a large group. It maybe a big corporation so they are all over the world. So it's going to get worse if we are not aware of it. They will continue to do their evil work. We need to stop this criminals by becoming smart of who are we talking to on the online dating. In fact, because they are very smart , they can write their own story of how they can trick you. Don't fall into their trap. If somewhere, somehow you make a decision that you will help them then make sure you will tell your friend or one of your family about it and tell the scammers of what you just did. You can tell that they are fraud because they don't like if you let other people know about it. These are the mistake that I made. I wasn't using my head; instead I was using my heart.

Most pictures that the scammers use are of people who are young and good-looking. They are using "glamour shots." This is the kind of picture posted for Gabriel, the man I was supposedly talking to. These people won't use ugly or unprofessional-looking pictures—be aware of this, because they know that ugly or ordinary people won't attract much attention. It is absolutely normal for us to be looking for someone whom we are attracted to. If a guy is posting as a good-looking man, he will also use the best profession for his picture, so women will see that he makes a lot of money as well as being handsome. If the profile created is for a woman, the photo of a young, good-looking woman is used. The predators know that the majority of older men want younger women to be their wives or girlfriends. The scammers are professional and are good at what they do. They master techniques so you won't be able to tell who is real and who is fake. They are master manipulators. They will put the best out there because it's a bait. The more responses they get to the profile, the more people they can lie to and victimize.

The scammers try to pursue you and make you believe that you will soon meet each other. They will do anything they can to make you give in and believe them. They will talk marriage if they have to. These "people" will do anything to convince you that they love or care about you, including telling stories that you haven't heard or read before. If they have to invest time in you, they will do it in order to get you hooked on them. They are very good at putting on this act, and most of the time you won't be able to tell that they are lying. Once you start believing in them, they will take advantage of you. They will make sure you have confidence in them and that you are ready to engage in a Relationship even if you have not met each other. They will make you fall in love.

As soon as the scammer knows they have gained your trust, they will start their tricks to get money from you. In some cases they will use other names of a person or an organization to get what they want. Some of them will create a website in order for you to send money to them. Sometimes they even use their own children, but the truth is they don't have children. It's all just an illusion. You probably won't know that you are actually talking to multiple people all assuming the same identity. You won't have any idea unless you talk to them on the phone all the time. Listening to the person's voice is very important. For example, if you are a man and you think you are talking to a beautiful woman, you might actually be talking to a man. These con artists know how to do this. If they mention other people—for example, an agent—ask them if you can have the agent's picture with the person in it. If they can't provide the picture, cut them off and stop communicating, because the next thing that will happen is you will be asked for money. They will start sending you texts, IM messages, e-mails, and even phone calls to tell you how much they care about you. This is what I experienced.

After conversing for a while, the man would text me that he loved me "to the moon and back." He would write a poem and send it to me. He would call me "baby" all the time, and "princess" most of the time. A couple of times I received a phone call while I was driving home from work, telling me that he could not sleep because he was thinking about me, and that he couldn't wait to put his arms around me. These are examples of the type of thing they will tell you to get you hooked. Then come the lies and promised. Once you get hooked by those sweet, loving, and caring words, they know you have already developed some kind of trust. Then they will act quickly. This time they will tell you that they have a problem. The majority of them work overseas. Then they will start talking about money. Of course, because you already feel something special for them, the more that you want to see them, the more anxious you become to know more about them. When you are in this situation, you feel excited, and you start expecting to hear from them all the time. You develop a feeling of compassion.

Because of this, they will play their trick,

asking you for money, or telling you that they need help, hoping you will volunteer to give them money. You will be lucky if they ask only for a couple hundred dollars. But they usually want a thousand or more. Remember, they will always have another party to receive the money. They will tell you to send it to someone else instead of directly to them. The reason for this is that the name you see in the profile is a fake name. They cannot provide ID for that name. Some of them will use a company name—anything, just to get the money. They might say that the person receiving the money is their agent; that is what happened to me.

As time went by, I found out that the agent was a banker who withdrew all the money I sent, and who would also get a share of that money, so it's all a conspiracy. In other words, the person who does all the work won't get a hundred percent of the profit. So think about it—there is a huge organization out there. Be wise, be smart, be aware of who you're talking to online. Use your head: THINK. I don't want you to be the victim of a scam.

Again, I'm not saying you should avoid online dating. I believe good people are still out there—you just have to be careful. In fact, a few of my friends met their husbands online. I believe that genuine and honest people still exist. We just have to be extra cautious about choosing one. After everything that has happened to me, I will join another dating site eventually. But this time I will be very careful. I've learned my lesson, and that is why I wanted to share my story. Hopefully it will have a positive impact on many people.

It is typical for scammers to disappear after they get what they want. I wrote and published my story not only for those people who are using those dating site but also for those people in general using the Internet for what reason it may be. Those con-artist are in the Internet as well. It don't matter in what area. They are there. Just be aware and be extra cautious when you go on line. This is the reason why I want to share my story.

CHAPTER **2**

How and When It Begin

MY STORY BEGAN in the month of June, which was when I decided to join an international dating site. My first few days as a member were very colorful. I received many e-mails from men ranging in age from twenty-eight (which is way too young for me) to seventy-six (which is way too old!). It was kind of exciting for me, talking to men from different countries all over the world. There were also quite a few Americans on the site, but the majority were from the UK. Many of them admired my pictures. I posted five different pictures in my profile. Many members commented "nice photo" or "beautiful picture." Only one of those photos was taken when I was in my late forties. The rest were current, taken the year I joined the site. They weren't glamour shots; I just used my iPhone to take the pictures, and most were taken after church, which was the best time, since I was already dressed up. I got a lot of compliments on my photos.

Then I started communicating with some of the men. The way this dating site worked, you could communicate with and browse all members even if you didn't pay anything. You could communicate with a member as long as he or she had an upgraded membership (meaning that they already paid), but if both of you are standard members, then you can't even see what messages are sent to you, but you can still browse. The first time I answered an e-mail, I was still a standard member. I remember this man e-mailed me and told me that he lived in the UK. He was a gold member of that dating site. He was my age. I told him that I was looking for companionship. Of course I introduced myself and said that I was looking for a serious relationship as well. I had been going back and forth e-mailing a few men on the site. I didn't count the men who were too young for me. One of the men who was interested in me was from Turkey, and another was from Korea, but I wasn't interested in them, so I stopped responding to them, although they kept contacting me for another two weeks after I stopped e-mailing them back. I was able to read their e-mails because they had both already upgraded their memberships. They were quite interested in knowing more about me, but I wasn't interested in them, so I ignored them. After a while, they finally stopped, since I didn't answer them back. Another guy from Turkey named Mark emailed me. He was a platinum member so I was able to read his emails even if my membership was only standard. In his profile he mention that he was born and raised in Europe but did not say that he was from Turkey which it was posted in his profile. He is also good looking. It says that he is an engineer in a big firm. We been emailing to each other at least a week off and on. Until the time I log back in again, I noticed that the place where he from changes. I wonder why suddenly became different but I did not bother to ask him. The following day I log back in, the country where he from changes again. This time he is from Los Angeles CA. I said wow!! This person changes countries like putting clothes on. Either he is confuse or he is just playing games so I stop communicating .

After a week or so as a standard member, I was contacted by a good-looking man named Gabriel, but I couldn't read his e-mail. I waited for a couple of days before I decided to upgrade for a month in order to see what he had written. Before writing back, I checked his profile, because I didn't know who he was. He just suddenly popped up. I was thinking maybe he did not log in to this dating site in quite awhile because once you don't logged back in for so may days no one will see your profile even if you are a member. So as if it appear that you are a new member to the website. But the truth is his picture probably in this dating site for years as a standard member. Like one of the guys from Canada emailed and told me that he'd been to this website off and on for four years. Wow! I do not want to be in the same dating site that long as I emailed him back. I said to him if I won't find anyone in six months I will delete my profile and go somewhere else. There are hundreds of dating sites to choose from. Maybe this is the reason why I haven't seen Gabriel because this scammers who use the picture might scattered his profile in various area to look for prey. Gabriel's picture stand out for the reason of the way it was taken. His pictures are professionally done and the way he got dressed in those picture he looked absolutely gorgeous. Whether he is wearing a suit or in a cargo shorts, to me he was the best looking man in that dating site. As if it was done intentionally for women to see. A good looking man who has a bachelor's degree. I have not seen his face even when I was browsing, which I did quite often. His profile said he was from Balbriggan, Ireland. He was very good-looking, and had a close resemblance to a famous actor. He was tall, dark, and very handsome. His profile said that he owned his own business, and was in management. He had a bachelor's degree, and had two children who didn't live with him. He was 53 years old, and looking for a woman up to ten years younger or older than he was. I was within his preferred age range. His profile was professional and well-done. Mine was direct and simple. At that time, I did not focus on how his profile was written, because he was the man of my dreams. He had posted five different pictures, and I could tell that they were professional photos, not taken from an iPhone or smartphone. This didn't stop me from talking to him—at the time, I didn't know any better. I liked him, I was infatuated, and I didn't have any negative thoughts when I started communicating with him, since there were no warning signs to make him suspicious.

Every time we talked online, he seemed like a very well-educated person. The phrasing in his e-mails seemed polished, almost like he was an expert at knowing what to say...but I didn't notice that at the time. I felt like I was a teenager again, especially when he started sending more e-mails saying that he was interested in getting to know me. One thing I noticed was that he was a very fast typist. He told me that I was beautiful. Then he asked me how recent my pictures were. I told him they were pretty recent, except for the one where I had long hair. I thanked him when he told me how pretty I was. I told him that I got a lot of compliments on my looks, especially from people who knew how old I was. I was in my late fifties, but most people thought I was in my early forties. I said that looking young was a blessing, but I didn't take it for granted. I took care of myself by eating right and getting regular exercise. I told him I drank lots of water every day and went to the doctor once a year. I didn't smoke, and I didn't drink more than maybe a glass of wine a couple of times a week with dinner. I even joked that maybe work made me look younger, since I worked all the time, and I worked long hours. I had a busy schedule and was in high demand in the OR department. He said you must look young because of good genes, and I said maybe.

I told him that I had received e-mails from other members. I was excited every time I read my messages, but the only thing I wasn't happy about was the time difference...most were eight to ten hours ahead, so while it was daylight for me, it was already late on their end, so I had to wait for the next day until they could communicate online. Lots of them wanted to talk while they were on the site. But Gabriel, from Ireland, e-mailed me regularly. Eventually I stopped communicating with the other members who also wanted to get to know me. There was one man from the UK who was very interested, and asked, "What's wrong with the men in Florida?" (That was where I lived...in Florida, the Sunshine State.) He wanted to know why men in Florida weren't interested in me, when I was such a beautiful lady. In fact, he told me that if he had a way to get to the States, and he would find a job and move here because of me. I did answer his message and thanked him for all the nice things he said about me, but he just wasn't my type.

In other words, my mind was already made up. I was already smitten by this good-looking man who had a glamorous picture. The days went by quickly for me. Soon my membership would expire, since I upgraded for only a month. I had to let Gabriel know that soon, I wouldn't be able to read his messages, since he was also a standard member. He told me that it would be better for us to communicate through our personal e-mail, and suggested that we chat using Yahoo! Messenger. So we started using our personal e-mail accounts to communicate.

CHAPTER 3

Getting to Know Each Other

ONE DAY HE told me that he wanted to chat on Yahoo! Messenger instead of on the dating site. He wanted me to accept him as a new contact. We had discussed communicating off the dating site, but it had been more than ten years since I used Yahoo! chat, and I didn't remember my password or username. I told him that these days, people used text, FaceTime, or Skype. He told me that he didn't have any gadgets to support those platforms, that he was still using a BlackBerry, but he got a computer, so he could e-mail me his Yahoo! ID and private e-mail address.

He also gave me his cell phone number,

which had a Chicago area code. I asked him
how he got a Chicago cell phone number...
did he live there? He explained that he got
that number because he often traveled in
the United States for business. He said he
traveled to many countries, and told me that
he owned a business that supplied leather
materials for big companies in the US. He
said he just got done signing a big contract,
and he was in New York at the airport when
he was talking to me on the phone. In fact,
he said he was at the airport waiting for his
flight to go back to Ireland. He said that because he acted as a middleman, he needed
to get busy when he got home. While he was
at the airport, he gave me all his Yahoo! information so we could chat. He told me that
his two kids were grown and lived in the UK
with his ex-wife. He said he used to live in the
UK but decided to go back to Ireland when
he got divorced. Then he said that after this
conversation I might not hear from him for
a while because it would take eight to ten
hours to get to Ireland, and he might have a

long layover. He said as soon as he got home, he would call me.

The following day when I got off work, I couldn't wait to hear his voice again, so I decided to call the cell phone number he gave me. He answered, and I asked him how his flight was. He said it was smooth, with no problems at all. While I was talking to him on the phone, he said it would be better to use Yahoo! because then we could talk all we wanted for free. Instead of going to my computer, I installed the messenger app on my cell phone. "This way I will know right away when he send me a message," I told him. From then on, we talked via IM most of the time, so there was a record of most of our conversations. We even called each other through the voice video.

One day while we were having our conversation, he said that his cleaning lady was supposed to come over to clean his house. He said that he really needed to have his house cleaned since he had been away for quite a while. Then he continued and said that sometimes the cleaning lady also cooked for him. He said he paid her well, and she'd been his employee for quite a while, and that she was very trustworthy. Then he asked if I wanted to see some of his pictures. I told him, "Absolutely; I would love to see them." So he sent me some pictures. In the pictures, I saw that he had two beautiful dogs. I asked him who watched them when he was away. He said that his cleaning lady took care of them when he was away for a short time, and otherwise his neighbors watched them.

One of the things he told me was that when he got married, he and his wife had their honeymoon in Hawaii. He said his ex wife works in a hospital in the Emergency Department as a doctor. He knows I worked in the medical field because he saw this in my profile, this probably the reason why he create this kind of profession for his wife. He is very clever and smart still I don't have any clue that I am talking to a con-artist. He told me the reason why they got divorce: because him and his wife don't get along in making major important decision when it comes to being married. One factor of the divorce is his profession being away all the time. That they constantly arguing over it. Majority of those times, when they argue the kids are there listening. He said he hates the fact that the children are involved so he made the decision to end the marriage. Now that they are separated they maintain a good relationship because of their children . He told me many different things, including how many times he traveled during the year. Most of the time, he was away from home. He said that he was constantly busy looking for new products. But most of the places he'd been, he had connections, so it wasn't hard on him when he got there. He said the most important thing was to meet the business demands for customers, because he signed a contract that his company would be a supplier of materials for leather products. During our conversation, he told me that he didn't like being in the office all the time, and he preferred to travel. I asked him who did the paperwork and took care of day-to-day issues for his company while he was gone, and he said he had a business partner, as well as his own secretary. I never had the slightest idea that these were all lies, since he knew exactly how to answer.

CHAPTER **4**

Start Falling and Believing the Lies

IT DIDN'T MATTER whether we talked on the phone or over the computer—the longer we talked, the more I developed feelings for him, and the more I liked and believed him. Then I asked him if he could send more pictures of him and his kids. He sent me at least fifteen more pictures. Somehow, the majority of the pictures looked as if he did not know that someone was taking his picture. They seemed like candid shots, but he was rarely looking toward the camera. I had all kinds of pictures—even pictures of him coloring or cutting his kids' hair in their back yard. Some pictures were of his family, his brother, dad, cousins, his colleagues, house, dogs, car, etc. It never occurred to me that he was a con artist. I thought he was honest because he told me so many things about himself.

He even told me about his plans for when his son graduated from college. He told me he wanted his son to take over the business. He said to me that he would train his son and nephew in business strategy, so they could take over, because he didn't want to spend all his time traveling anymore. He said he was getting older, and it would be very difficult for him to keep running around in the jungle looking for and inspecting the products. Then he said to me that once he found the right woman, he would get married again, and he didn't want to be away from his wife for long periods of time once he was married. He wanted to spend most of his time with his wife. Honestly, I was thrilled when he told me all these things. I felt like I was dreaming, and I didn't want to wake up. I never had a clue as to what would happen in the long run.

Time went by, and we had been talking to each other for more than a month. I was getting excited to know more and more about him. His messages always brought a smile to my face. I ended up telling him what I did for a living. I told him that I might not be making millions every day when I went to work, but I was very proud of what I did when it came to my job. I told him, "I work in a place where we help people to get better when there is something seriously wrong with their health." I told him I worked in one of the OR departments at a well-known hospital in Florida. He was amazed when he found out what I do. He said that was not the kind of profession he could get into, because he didn't like blood. I told him, "It's not for everyone, but I like helping people, and I work with a lot of good people, as well."

Then I asked him again, "What are the kids doing now? How old are they?" He said that the kids were finishing school—his daughter, who was seventeen, was getting ready to graduate from high school, and his son, who was twenty, was in college. He said that he had been married for ten years, and he told me again that he didn't like the idea of being far away from his kids, but he needed to go back home and take care of his grandfather's failing business. He went back to restore the business instead of only supplying locally to companies in his area. He wanted to be an international supplier of leather products. He said every time the kids were out of school, he would be in the UK so he could spend time with them. Sometimes, he told me, the kids would come over to be with him in the summer. He said he always made time to be with his kids. I told him that I admired him for being a good father, even if he and his wife were separated.

He told me that both of his parents died in a car accident a long time ago, and that he and his brother grew up with their grandparents. When he told me this story, I said I had grown up in the same situation; my grandparents also raised me, but my grandma died when I was only four years old. I didn't have any parents when I was growing up.

After this conversation, Gabriel sent me more love notes every day. Sometimes he would send me a text or IM telling me how much he enjoyed having a conversation with me. Then he started sending me poems. Sometimes he sent me a musical card—the ones you can get from the internet. He would e-mail them to me. He called me "princess" all the time. A couple of times, he sang to me over the phone. He had a beautiful voice that I told him he should be a professional singer. He said he wanted to when he was younger, but now it seemed too late because he was getting old. I admit that I was overwhelmed with joy. Every time my phone made any kind of noise, I expected it to be him. There was a six-hour time difference between Florida and Ireland, so his night was my day, and vice versa. There was never a dull moment when Gabriel and I were talking. He was full of life when it came to our conversations.

CHAPTER 5

His Trip to Morocco and Kenya

THEN ONE DAY he said that his business partner received a phone call from one of their agents in Morocco, telling them that there were some products for them to purchase in that country. He said he had to go there in a couple of days to check on the animal skins that were the material for leather. Once he got to Morocco and got settled, he said, he wanted me to join him so we could meet. He said I didn't have to worry about my plane ticket; he would pay for it. All I would have to do was arrange for my passport or other necessary documents. I told him I had a current passport, and my own research told me it wasn't difficult to get to Morocco as long as I had a valid US passport.

When he asked me to join him in Morocco, I wasn't interested. I had met quite a few Moroccans where I worked, and although they seemed nice, I didn't want to go there. I did not tell him that. Instead, I kept giving different excuses. I felt it was too dangerous for me to travel to that country. I heard that in Morocco, you are not allowed to kiss in public, but you can hold hands while walking. I was worried about what would happen if he forgot and kissed me. I was worried about the fact that the women there covered their faces, and about not knowing anyone or having enough time to prepare for the trip. While the men are allowed to have three or four wives. It scare me after knowing that as well. But before he flew to Morocco, he said that he had received another phone call from his agent in Kenya, who said that there were more products in Kenya than in Morocco. I was relieved. I said, "Wow, you have these agents everywhere!" He said they got their animal skins from only three countries: Morocco, Kenya, and Venezuela. They had a personal agent in each country who would notify his company when products were available so that he could make a trip to inspect the products as soon as possible. As soon as he could gather enough skins, his company would send them to China for processing.

Gabriel said that he had to change his plans, and he would go to Kenya instead of to Morocco. After the call from his agent, he said he was going to have a meeting with his partner and secretary so that they could arrange the trip. He said he had to choose the country that had more product for him to buy, so his trip wouldn't be a waste. Once again, he invited me to join him. He said that he would like to get settled first, and then I could come over and join him. Since his agent was already there, he said, it wouldn't take long for him to get a good, decent place to stay. He said it would take a month or two to do his business, and then ship everything to China. Then he would go back to Ireland. If everything worked out and went smoothly, then he would spend only a month or two working in each country. He said we would have plenty of quality time together while he was in Kenya, even if he was working. He said that if I were there, he would let his agent do the work so he could spend time with me. But he said that he wouldn't mind going to the jungle to look for products. He and his agent, Michael, traveled together because Michael knew most of the best places to get leather.

A day or two went by after he got to Kenya, and then he sent me a message with the name of the hotel where he was staying. He was in a suite at the Prestige Hotel in Nairobi. As soon as I found out the name of the hotel, I Googled it. The same day, I called him on his cell phone. We talked for a little bit, and then he told me that we needed to talk online. He said he would get a Kenyan cell phone in case I wanted to reach him immediately. He said that whenever I wanted to come over, he was ready. Everything was situated. He said there was nothing to worry about, since he was staying in Nairobi, the capital of Kenya. He said he was staying in an area with a lots of tourists—there were even a lot of Asian people, mostly Koreans. He told me that he could hardly wait for me to come over so we could finally meet. He said his agent would arrange my plane ticket and e-mail it to me; all I had to do was make the decision to go. He told me over and over not to worry about terrorists, that there weren't any in Nairobi. There was bombing, but only outside the city.

I wasn't sure if I wanted to go. Kenya was another place that wasn't on my list of places to visit. I didn't tell him that I had the same feeling I'd had when he asked me to meet him in Morocco. So far, I was not comfortable going to those countries. Maybe it was because every time I told my friends about those places, they told me it wasn't safe and I shouldn't go. I didn't tell him the truth, that I was afraid to visit those countries. Instead, I said to him, "In case I come over, I would like my own room in the same hotel." He laughed and said it would be a waste of money, because he was paying for it. He said I didn't have anything to worry about because he was a good person and not a criminal—he hadn't killed anyone.

Another factor to consider was the long trip to get there...and also, I didn't really know this man. He seemed to be a very thoughtful, caring, and loving person, and he was a Christian. But that wasn't the point. We'd been talking for only a month or so. I wasn't ready to meet him yet.

I found out he was a Christian because he told me that every Sunday he went to church with his agent's family. Sometimes in our conversations he told me that if he was not working, he was reading a book by an evangelical preacher. I believed him because most Irish people are Catholic, and also we had nuns from Ireland where I worked. I replied that every Sunday before I went to church, I would pray for him so the Lord would keep him safe and protect him from harm while he was in Kenya. I thought everything he said was real, especially what he said about church and God. Who would have thought it was all lies? I think he just wanted me to trust him before he started on his real purpose. He really did a good job of misleading me. I was not aware of his tricks because I was not using my head. I wasn't thinking. I was overwhelmed by my feelings for him. He told me that once we got together, he would want me to move to Ireland to be with him for good, so we didn't have to keep going back and forth between two countries. I told him maybe that would happen, but it would depend on how our relationship went, and I wanted to be retirement age before I made a decision to move. He told me that there was nothing to worry about because his house was paid off in Ireland. These things were all too good to be true, but I believed him. I thought his intentions were sincere.

He continued to send me love notes. One morning I woke up and heard my phone; sure enough, it was Gabriel sending me a text. He said, "Good morning, Princess. How are you?" I saw a different number this time. He told me to be sure I had that number with me all the time, because it was the number he would be using in Kenya. He wanted me to call him at that number when I got to the airport in Kenya. At that time I didn't know any better. I didn't know that he deliberately did that in order to make me believe that he really wanted to meet me. The truth was that he already planned to deceive me in so many different ways. He wanted to make sure I would feel comfortable with him, so that I would trust and believe him. This was before I found out everything he was doing.

On one occasion, he wanted me to open a bank account for him in the US. I asked him why he hadn't opened one the last time he was here. I didn't know how that would work, since he was a foreigner. I told him that on his next trip, he should go to a bank personally and inquire about it. He asked me why I couldn't do it. I told him I would probably need all of his information, including a valid ID. When I mentioned that, he immediately said that we would have to talk about it some other time.

The chances of my going to Kenya were very slim. I didn't know the whole truth, but even though I really wanted to meet him, I wasn't planning to go there. At that time, I was already planning a trip to Europe, to visit six different countries.

CHAPTER **6**

The Accident

A WEEK WENT by and then one day when we were online, Gabriel told me his secretary had e-mailed him to say that his partner had been in a bad motorcycle accident. It had happened that weekend. He said his partner was in the ICU at a hospital in Dublin, and the doctors said the prognosis was not good. His friend and family didn't know whether he would survive, and he was in a coma. Even if he did survive, he might not be able to work again. Gabriel told me that he had been worried about his company, so he needed to hurry up and complete his business, and go back home. Before he received the bad news, he told me that if

I wasn't able to join him in Kenya, he would come to the United States before going back to Ireland, and he would spend a couple of days with me here. He said that when he got here, he wouldn't have time to run around, and he would want to rest. I told him that I would plan to take him to a few places so that he would enjoy his stay. He said that wouldn't be necessary, because he had already been to Florida when he visited his nephew who lived in Fort Lauderdale.

I believed him, and I was thrilled that he would make the sacrifice to come to the United States to see me. I felt very happy. I was compassionate when he told me that his partner was in the hospital. I told him that he needed to go home and not worry about visiting me in Florida. I told him he needed to attend to his priorities first. I felt that I had to do something to comfort him, so I said that I would cancel my European tour, and instead I would come to see him in Ireland when he got back home. He said I would be more than welcome, but that he had an obligation to fulfill and he needed to finish what he'd started before he could go back, because he signed a contract to be a materials supplier for other companies, and that if he didn't honor that contract, he'd be in trouble. He said that once he got home, he might be looking for a new business partner, if his partner in the hospital didn't get better He said it would be hard to find a partner he could trust who knew the ins and outs of the business, and that his current partner was really smart. The only thing he didn't like about him was his partner's boyfriend (his partner was gay) who tried to interfere in how the company was run. He told me that a couple of times they had a big discussion about it, and they almost ended their partnership because of the argument. But other than that, his business partner was great, especially when it came to running the business while Gabriel was away.

Time went by quickly for Gabriel. He had already been in Kenya for nearly two months and soon he would run out of money—that is what he told me. He still needed to buy more materials, and he didn't have enough money to send the products to China. He told me that he wanted to buy the materials from an Indian guy, but he didn't have any US currency. When Gabriel told me about this, I suggested that he convert his money to US currency. Immediately after my suggestion, he said they wouldn't do that in Kenya, that it was impossible to convert Kenyan currency to the US dollar; nobody would do it. He really wanted to buy the products from this Indian Guy because he always had top-quality animal skins, and he wouldn't accept Kenyan currency. He said that even though he had been dealing with him for a while, the Indian guy wouldn't compromise.

Then Gabriel asked if he could borrow money from me. He said he would pay me back as soon as he returned to Ireland. We had been talking for almost two months before Gabriel asked for money from me. I accused him of making up this story so that he could get money from me. I asked him if this was a scam. He got really mad and sent me a long e-mail saying that he himself was the victim of a scam. He said that I had insulted him, and he was deeply hurt by my accusation. He said that in Ireland, he owned his house and gave money to charity. He said he was supposed to see his children during summer vacation, but because of the situation, he wouldn't be able to see them, and now I was making things worse by calling him a scam artist. He said that he already felt bad that he wouldn't be seeing his children, and now thanks to my accusation he felt even worse. Then he said that if I wouldn't lend him the money, he would have to find some other way to pay for the product, because he needed to be able to ship it to China at once; his time was very limited.

Because of my strong feelings for Gabriel, I asked him to forgive me for calling him a scam artist. It did not take long for him to accept my apology—because, he said, he really cared for me. He wanted us to be together. Therefore, as we continued our conversation, he mentioned getting married and buying an expensive diamond ring. I said, "This is not the most important thing right now." I told him I didn't need an expensive ring. I told him I was not after his money, and I wasn't after the other material things he mentioned. The most important thing to me was being with him. He told me he loved me even more because of what I'd said, and he wanted us to be together.

The following morning, he told me that he and his agent had to go to Mombasa, Africa. His agent Michael received information that there was more product in that area for them if they wanted to buy. Gabriel told me that he and his agent would be leaving soon. He would make a deal again with the Indian when he got back. After five hours or so, I received a text from him telling me the name of the hotel where he was staying He said they would stay there for at least three days, so he had to put the other goods that he already purchased in a warehouse. He said he wanted to wait and ship it all together to save money.

CHAPTER 7

Falling into the Trap

THIS TIME, I decided that I wanted to help him. I really wanted him to be able to purchase the product. So I told him that I would let him borrow money from me as long as he promised to pay me back. He said he would repay me with interest, as soon as he got back to Ireland. As I was getting ready to send him the money, he told me to send it to his agent. I asked why I would do that, when I didn't know the agent and had never spoken to him. Gabriel said he trusted Michael because he had been Gabriel's employee for years. He was from Kenya, he went to church regularly, and he had a wife and three children. He told me that if there were any problem collecting the money, Michael would be able to do it more easily because he had connections. He told me there was nothing to worry about, and I should send the money to Michael. But I refused, and I sent it to Gabriel.

I found out from Gabriel that he was having a problem getting the money. He told me to call Western Union and cancel the transaction, which I did, and I received a refund. After I got the refund, I did not ask why he could not collect the money. Instead, I went ahead and sent it a second time, through Western Union, in Michael's name. In a couple of hours he called and told me he had the money. He thanked me for helping him. I did not have a clue that Gabriel's name was made-up, and he couldn't collect the money because there was no ID that existed for that name.

All of this happened on a Friday, so I asked what he was going to do for the rest of the weekend, since he already had most of the product and he wouldn't have to work. He told me he planned to take a break—he and his agent might go see a movie, or maybe he would play golf so he could relax and not think about his problems. Since he mentioned movies, I told him about the movie *Heaven Is for Real.* I told him I had gone to see it. He said it wasn't in theaters yet in Kenya, so they went to play golf instead. I told him to send me some pictures. He sent me six different pictures of himself playing golf. I was so stupid…I didn't ask why his agent wasn't in any of the pictures. It didn't cross my mind to ask why nobody else was in the photos with him, because I was so blinded by my feelings for him. In other words, I was overwhelmed, and I can't deny that he always put a smile on my face.

One day during our conversation I asked whether he really was the co-owner of his company. He said, "Yes. Why are you asking stupid questions? Why are you doubting me?" I told him that if he was the co-owner of his company, he should have access to a lot of things, including company accounts to get money in case of emergency. He said it wasn't that simple, since his partner was in a coma, and Gabriel was in a foreign country, and their company accounts had been hacked in the past via the internet. The bank would give him a hard time about transferring the funds. The only way he could get more money was to tell his secretary to go to the bank and try to make a withdrawal from his personal account. He also told me that his secretary offered to gather more money for him to help him out. He said he had e-mailed the bank to explain what was going on, and he told his secretary to let the bank call him if she had a problem, because it was very important for him to pay these people so he could ship the product to China. He also told me that his sister-in-law was getting money together for his day-to-day expenses, but his bills kept coming, so it would be a wise decision to move to a cheaper room instead of staying in a suite.

One day before I went to work I received a phone call from him telling me that the people who were supposedly shipping the product agreed to ship everything as long as he made a promise to pay them as soon as he received the money from his bank, but with a condition:

he had to let the authorities hold his passport as collateral so he wouldn't flee the country without paying. He said he didn't like this idea, but he didn't have a choice. His deadline had to be met. What worried him was that if he didn't get the money soon enough, the product wouldn't get to its destination on time if he wouldn't agree to what they told him to do. I told him that as a businessman it didn't matter; as I explained, he should be ready, and he should have brought enough money with him, or had a credit card, or money available in case of emergency. He said he had brought money and credit cards, but his partner was supposed to wire him more cash while he was there in Kenya if he needed it. That was the plan. He said he did not expect any of this to happen, since he traveled all the time.

While he was waiting, Gabriel told me that he downsized his room at the hotel. He had been staying in a suite before, and he moved to a regular room to save money. He said that as soon as he got what he needed, he would go home to Ireland so he could take care of the problems waiting for him. Every now and then, I asked him how his partner was doing. Gabriel said he just received an e-mail from his partner's boyfriend saying that his partner was still in a coma, and his situation was getting worse. He said to me that there was really nothing he could do but pray and wait for the rest of the money. He said he had enough money to pay for all the product, because of the money I sent him, but not enough to pay for the shipping.

Now that I know the truth, I realize the reason he was telling me all this was because there was no bank account and he didn't own a company. Everything he had said to me was a lie. But before the truth came out, I admit it never occurred to me that the things he had been saying were not true, and that he'd made everything up. He did an excellent job of lying. Every time we talked on the phone, he maintained such a pleasant conversation that it seemed like we'd known each other for a very long time. All I know is that when my phone rang or made any noise, I'd jump, excited and happy to hear from him. I began to expect contact from him—it didn't matter whether it was a call or a text, or him singing to me over the phone; he became like a part of me. I thought about him daily, especially when he called me before I went to work. Sometimes he would sing to me on the phone. He had a beautiful voice, and sang American songs. In fact, he mentioned lots of American singers. He told me he loved just about all kinds of music. He even mentioned the singer "Bob Marley" that he loves his music. I replied at him and said, before you love Bob Marley I love him first. Then he laugh. He said he loved country-western music as well. I was always amazed that he knew so many popular singers. I told him I loved listening to him sing, and asked why he didn't become a singer. I told him that I loved to sing as well. I used to play the guitar when I was growing up. We had so many different conversations…I felt as if I'd known him all my life. So often I will ask him what is he going to do when he is not working. Most of the time he told me that he is just relaxing drinking Hennessy in the balcony of the hotel. Watching the people go by. I don't know nothing about drinks. So I did not have a clue that most black people drinks Hennessy. Sometimes he will tell me that there is a bar in the hotel so he will just stay there and have a drink. The brand of his drink is a hint about his identity, but I don't know nothing about liqueur. Therefore, I pretty much don't have any idea who he really is at this point. A few times during our conversation he will tell me that after he'd done working, he will do his "Self Development ."Not sooner than I think, what self development I'd ask. He said it's not important for me to know. Is it self development to become an expert as a liar? Or self development to become an expert as a scammer? This is before I knew everything. So we continue our conversation without me knowing that he is a con- artist. I also asked him the name of his company. He gave me this abbreviation .(O.O.V.N.O.S) I asked what it means , he said he cannot tell me yet because I am not part of the family yet. So I did not bother to ask about it anymore since he does not like for me ask him over and over. It was amazing, the way we could talk to each other. We talked all the time, but we had never met.

In those days, when he got frustrated, he would always tell me why he felt that way. Most of the time I told him to pray and talk to God, and hand it all to Him if it was too much to handle. I told him that I prayed all the time— God and prayers were all I had. I told him I said a prayer first thing in the morning, and in the evening before I went to bed. I mentioned to him that I always thanked our Lord Jesus Christ for all the blessings He'd given me. In other words, I talked to God daily. Sometimes, if I were having a hard day, I had to pray that I could make good choices, rather than letting my feelings run my life. All of us are dealing with different issues in our lives, and I'm no different from anyone else. I told Gabriel that instead of worrying, he needed to pray and talk to our Lord Jesus Christ. He said that all his life, he had believed there was a God. I told him I believed that, too. I told him that from the first day we started talking, I prayed for him, that the Lord would protect whatever he does, wherever he goes. I told him that I said a prayer for him every time I went to church. He thanked me and said he appreciated everything I did.

Since then, having a conversation with him was just a normal part of my day. Every day he would text me and call me "princess." Even if he was having a problem, he still tried to tell me that soon we would be together. That was what I had been told by him—that we would meet each other soon. It inspired me every time he told me this, and all I knew was that I looked forward to it. Then he sent me more pictures of himself, so I sent more as well. This time the pictures were mostly from work. When he sent me pictures of himself and his older brother (at least, that's who he claimed it was) I asked him where his brother was now. He said he lived in South Africa with his wife and kids. He also said that his brother had a stroke a couple of years ago, and had a hard time walking, so he used a wheelchair. He said every now and then he would visit his brother if he was not traveling, because it was hard for his brother to travel due to his illness.

Every day, Gabriel would tell me that he loved me. I imagined what it would be like to be with him when the time came. I couldn't help but wonder whether he was really this loving and thoughtful. I often asked myself whether this could be real. Would he still call me by all those sweet names? Whatever was happening, I loved the way I felt. It was almost like a dream, and I hated the thought of waking up. I had no clue that a bombshell was going to explode.

On the weekend we usually talked for hours, especially when he knew that I didn't have any plans to go anywhere. The eight-hour time difference was nothing to him. He would stay up and talk to me until dawn. We talked about who would move—me or him, since he was in Ireland and I was in the US. It was all too good to be true.

A week went by, and Gabriel had been in Kenya for more than two months. He mentioned again that the longer he stayed, the more money he needed, because of daily living costs. He said that as soon as he got money from his secretary, he would give the money to the company to ship the products to China. Finally I received a message from him telling me that he got the money from his secretary. All he needed now was the money from his brother's wife. I told him that I was happy for him—at last he got what he was waiting for, and that was good news. He said he was able to get his passport back, so he could go home to Ireland. The sooner he got back, the better it would be. He told me that as soon as he got home, he would pay me. He reminded me again that he would pay not just the amount he borrowed; he would pay me back with interest. I told him that I had let him borrow without interest. He thanked me, as usual. He said that he appreciated my helping him, from the bottom of his heart. Then he suggested that I go to Ireland to see him. I said immediately that I would be glad to.

CHAPTER 8

My Trip to Ireland

I WAS VERY excited. It didn't take long for me to research whether I needed a visa to visit Ireland. I was very interested in going this time, especially since Ireland was one of the countries I had already wanted to visit. I found out that I could get a visa at the airport once I arrived there, as long as I had a US passport. I wanted to get going so I could do some sight-seeing while Gabriel was still in Kenya. I was very excited about preparing for this trip, so I cancelled my six-country tour. I told him that I would stay in a hotel for a couple of days while waiting for him to arrive. As I said to him, I had already been planning to visit Ireland,

and finally this was the opportunity I had been waiting for. Gabriel agreed with my plans. He said it would be fine if I got there first—he just reminded me to be careful. Before I gathered the necessary things I needed for my trip , I ask him who will meet me in the airport. He said not a problem. One of his closest friend will pick me up. I booked my plane ticket, made my hotel reservation online, and made the necessary arrangements, including taking time off from work. I asked for ten days off— that way I would have enough time to explore Ireland and still spend time with Gabriel when he arrived.

As soon as I purchased my plane ticket, I e-mailed him with my travel details. I was staying at a hotel not too far from the airport. He told me he knew that hotel, and it had nice rooms—some of his friends from the UK had stayed there before. He said there was nothing to worry about, and he would e-mail me his ticket details as soon as he got the ticket from his agent, since he was the one who arranged all his travel details. But first he had to take care of the mess he'd gotten into. On our conversation I told him that it is not necessary for his friend to pick me up. That I just get a taxi from the airport to the hotel. And he agree. This time, my heart was pounding with excitement. Finally, I would see him in person, as well as taking the vacation of my dreams. Because of my excitement, I dreamed about the trip at night.

The day of my flight, I texted Gabriel telling him that I was on my way to the airport. As I was waiting for my flight to board, I received a message from him that the amount of money his secretary sent was a little bit short. In other words, he wanted to borrow more money from me. I was still blinded by my feelings for him, so I told him I would send him the money when I got to Ireland. I thought and assumed that soon he would be back home anyway, and he would pay me back. When I got to Ireland and was in the cab going to my hotel, the driver asked me why I wanted to stay at this hotel, which was rather far from the city of Dublin. He said I could have gotten a hotel within walking distance of everything. I told him that it was my first time in Ireland, and I would be in the hotel for only a couple of days, since I was waiting for someone. He asked me whether I was waiting for someone from Ireland, and I said yes. Gabriel had given me his address and e-mailed me his passport because I asked him to. I wanted to know if he really had his passport. My mind was like a roller coaster...I was full of excitement that finally I would get to meet his man that I had been talking to.

As soon as I checked in at my hotel, I got a taxi cab, and asked the driver if he knew where I could find a Western Union in Dublin. The driver was so nice. He drove me to so many places where he had seen Western Union, but none of them were open. He stopped and asked someone, and they said that the Western Union was inside the post office. The driver took me to a post office, which was inside a grocery store. The taxi driver told me he wouldn't charge anything to wait for me, so I went inside. There was a long line, and only two people working. I wanted to do this for Gabriel, though. When finally it was my turn, somehow the computer wasn't working correctly. The person who was helping me called Western Union, and still she couldn't make her computer work.

I am a very superstitious person—and I wondered if this might be a sign not to send the money. But I wanted to send it anyway. So I had to wait for the other employee to do it on her computer. Finally on the third try, it worked. I don't want to disclose the amount I sent, but it was enough to go back and forth to Ireland three more times. I believed that soon I would see Gabriel and get my money back. The taxi driver was waiting for me patiently, so I gave him a tip, but he wouldn't accept it. He was such a nice, good-hearted person. During my stay in Ireland, I found that the Irish are very nice and friendly.

The day went by, and I didn't waste my time waiting for Gabriel to come home. I went and purchased a ticket to go on a tour with a group. I didn't want to ruin my trip. I made the deci- sion to just enjoy waiting for Gabriel. I didn't want to stay inside the hotel doing nothing. I went out to eat. I went shopping. I even tried the famous homemade ice cream (gelato). I did enjoy myself. Ireland is a beautiful country, and the people are very friendly. I even went to have a drink of Guinness, their famous beer. I rode a double-decker bus, and sat on top. I went to this church, St. Patrick's, the first deacon in that church is buried inside. Ireland is famous of many old and beautiful churches. I enjoyed my stay even though Gabriel wasn't there.

Finally, he sent me the information for his flight reservation. I should have been happy and excited, but I felt rather awkward. I felt funny, as if something bad was going to happen. That night before I went to bed, I prayed God to ease my feelings. But still I couldn't sleep. So I called Gabriel on the phone from my hotel room. I told him that I had a funny feeling. He told me to ignore it, so I listened to him. The next day, I woke up early, so I would have enough time to get ready and check out of the hotel. I didn't want to be late picking up Gabriel from the airport. I arrived an hour early. I had my luggage with me, since I'd already checked out of the hotel. I was thinking that if anything went wrong, I would just get a hotel closer to where he lived.

There were so many flights that day from London—that was where the airline transferred from Kenya. I had been waiting hours and hours...but no Gabriel. I went to the information desk, to ask whether I'd missed his flight. The people at the desk wouldn't tell me whether he was on that flight; they said it was confidential information. It was getting late and I was tired. I was thinking that Gabriel wouldn't show up, that he'd lied to me. Therefore I made the decision to leave, because it was already getting dark. He was supposed to arrive a little after noon. I was devastated and disappointed, and tired from waiting all day. I decided to leave the airport because it was late, and no more flights were scheduled to arrive from London that night. The next incoming flight would be early in the morning. I was very confused and wanted to know what was really going on. I didn't know what to do, except pray to God to protect me and give me strength. I couldn't think straight, because I was tired and hurt and very disappointed.

I had to get another cab. I made a decision while in the cab to tell the driver to take me to the address that Gabriel gave me. I looked at the address and saw it said Dublin, although his profile said he was located in Balbriggan. Still, I wanted to find out what was going on, even if I was very tired and confused. When we got to the address, the cab driver and I knocked at the door. A lady answered, and I showed her Gabriel's picture from my iPad. She said that he didn't live there, and while she was talking to us, she remarked that his pictures looked too professional...like they had been produced by a studio. I turned around and I couldn't help crying while I asked the driver to help me look for another hotel because I had already checked out of the last one. The driver felt sorry for me as he drove me around. My luck had run out; every hotel we went to was fully booked. I thought I would have to sleep on a bench that night. There was a big game going on in Dublin, which was why the hotels were busy. I couldn't control myself; I cried more and more, and the driver told me that he would not stop looking until we found somewhere for me to stay. It was getting darker outside. The fifth hotel we tried had a couple of rooms available. I thanked God as I went inside. I was so glad, and so was the taxi driver. He wished me good luck, and then he left. I checked in, and I told the receptionist what had happened to me. She felt bad for me and asked whether I wanted to talk to the police. I said yes. I didn't know that the police station was very close to the hotel. So she called the police station and then told me to wait in my room.

CHAPTER 9

Fear of Knowing the Truth

WHILE I WAS waiting for the police to come, I tried to call Gabriel on his phone, but there was no answer. I called again and again. I must have called twenty times, but the phone was on voicemail. I cried and cried in the hotel room. Then around 7:30 p.m. the cops finally came. There were two of them, one female and one male. They were both nice. I explained to them everything that had happened. The cops asked if I had Gabriel's picture, his flight reservation, and a copy of his passport, and I said yes. I told them I had all of that saved on my iPad. They took all the information about him, and they got my information too. They said they would run an investigation...that this type of scam happened a lot in Ireland, too. They told me that many Irish men and women reported that they were being victimized by a scam—especially women. They told me they felt sorry for me, and they hated to know this had happened to me in their country. The male cop said it would take at least three weeks to a month for the investigation. I also had Gabriel's old flight information and a phone number from Ireland.

As we were talking, the male cop called their office to find information for that phone number, but they couldn't find anything. The phone number was not registered. They also said they would send Gabriel's passport for investigation in London. Then the male cop asked for my e-mail address. He gave me his e-mail as well as his address where they worked. After the cops left that night, I made the decision not to spend the rest of my vacation in Ireland. I had taken ten days off work because I thought it would be nice to spend time with Gabriel. In fact, we talked all about it before I went on my trip. I decided to cut my trip short, since I already saw what I needed to see in Ireland, and I was glad I'd enjoyed some of it. In spite of the disappointment and fear regarding Gabriel, I did not regret going to Ireland. The country was absolutely beautiful, and the people were great. I wouldn't mind going back again. In fact, while I was there, most of the taxi drivers who drove me around Dublin said that they had visited the United States, and loved our country. They said that we were blessed, because we have everything. It was raining and cold when I was in Ireland, and I barely saw any sunshine. But the United States has mountains, plains, beautiful parks, rain, sunshine, and snow...we have forests, and most of all, we have space everywhere. Irish people don't have a lot of these things. Their space is very limited. When I went to church on Sunday to attend Mass at St. Mary's in Dublin, I heard the priest talking about New York. The Irish really loved the United States!

Although I didn't regret going to Ireland, I didn't want to spend the rest of my vacation days alone. So I changed my flight the second day I spent at the hotel. After a week in Ireland, I went home. I still hadn't heard anything from Gabriel. I did not call him. Instead, I e-mailed him asking why he did what he had done. I let him know everything that had happened when he did not show up. I told him that I cut short my vacation and went home. It was a week before I heard from him. He told me that he got really sick the day before his flight—he was throwing up and had a high fever. This happened during the Ebola virus outbreak. He said that he had to go to the emergency room, and they kept him for observation. I didn't know how good the hospitals were in Kenya—maybe not as good as our hospitals in the States. I had serious doubts about whether he was telling me the truth.

I decided not to go back to work, since I still had a few days off. I prayed most of the time for God to ease my ugly feelings. I prayed that God would show me and direct me to the truth. Then one night I dreamed about Gabriel. I dreamed that we saw each other. He was tall and good-looking in my dream, just like he was in his profile. The dream was so real, but I didn't know what it meant.

Suddenly, Gabriel communicated with me again through Yahoo! Messenger. He told me that he needed help with his hospital bills. He said that the doctor had prescribed some medicines, but he didn't have the money to pay for the prescriptions, and his hospital bills were staggering. As I said early in my story, I had developed special feelings for this man. But this time, I was afraid. Deep inside, I knew he was lying to me. But something told me to continue communicating with him, even though I had mixed feelings. I didn't tell him that I had gone to the address he gave me. Once again, he asked to borrow money. When I heard the word "borrow," an idea struck me like lightning. "All right then," I said, "I will help you again." But I told him there was a condition: instead of sending him the money, I would come over in person to Kenya and give him the money. I also told him that I wanted to see his hospital bills. Gabriel did not say a word when

I told him I would come to see him in Kenya. I already knew that he didn't believe I would go to that country, since he'd asked me before and I refused. But I was preparing for another trip, and this time it was for real.

CHAPTER **10**

Preparing for My Trip to Kenya

BEFORE I PURCHASED my ticket, I asked around and talked to people who had been to Kenya before. I got some information that it wasn't bad at all, and that if I liked to see animals, it was the best place to go—I could go on safari, which sounded great to me. I also knew some people that had been there. They said its not a bad place to visit. All I needed to do was stay in the Nairobi area, where the US Embassy was also located. That sounded like a good plan; if something bad happened, I could go to the embassy for help. I wanted to be prepared. I requested more days off from work, which were granted. The only part I didn't like was getting shots—the good thing was that most of the shots I had to get to work in the OR were still good, so I had to get only malaria and tetanus shots.

Next, I made my hotel reservation. Originally I wanted to stay at the Hilton, and the only thing stopping me was that they wouldn't give me a refund if I changed my mind about going, since they were running some kind of special promo for customers who would stay there that particular month, around the beginning of fall. Staying at the Hilton would be great, but I wasn't sure whether I would really go ahead with the trip or not…I was having some funny feelings about it. So in case I changed my mind, I wanted to be able to get my money back. I made a reservation at another hotel, not far from the Hilton. I even ask Gabriel to check the hotel for me to whether it is a good one or not. And then I made my flight reservation.

The following day, I told Gabriel I was ready for my trip, and that I had taken care of all the necessities. I didn't know that he still didn't believe I would go, because before, I wouldn't agree to go to Kenya even if he offered to pay for my plane ticket. But then again, I didn't know the truth. My closest friends discouraged me from going, because of the terrorists. But this time I was very serious about going, so I didn't tell anyone— nobody at work, and none of my friends. As soon as I had everything that I needed for the trip, I told Gabriel, and e-mailed him my flight information and the hotel reservation. He asked repeatedly if I was really coming over. I told him this time it was for real, and I would not change my mind; I was on my way to see him, and I would bring money for the hospital bills. The day before I left, Gabriel asked me the same questions over and over. I asked him why he kept repeating himself. In the past, if I forgot something we already discussed, he didn't like it when I asked again. So why was he asking me over and over now?

I asked if he would be able to meet me at

the airport. He said he would try, and asked me what I would be wearing. I said I would be wearing blue jogging pants with a white top, and white NIKE shoes. He even laughed and said, "Oh, you're ready to run!" and I said yes. I also told him that I had the US Embassy's number just in case, and that the embassy building was only a block away from my hotel. But I was only making a joke when I said I was ready to run. Then he said, "This time, it's for real," and he got very quiet. I didn't know what was on his mind. Then he said to call him again before I left the house for the airport.

That night before I went to bed, I prayed about my trip. I hoped the Lord would protect me and keep me safe. I'd never been to this country, and even though I heard that there was nothing to worry about, I couldn't help thinking about danger. I wasn't excited as I was when I went to Ireland. When I went to bed that night, I tried to sleep, but I couldn't. Around 4:00 a.m. I heard my phone. It was Gabriel asking me if I was really coming to Kenya. I said, "Absolutely. I am ready. There is no backing out." There was a pause, and then for a while he didn't say anything. Then he said, "Abort, abort—change your plans." I was very surprised. I asked him why. He said he didn't want me to come. I asked him again and again why not. My heart was pounding...I was so confused. I didn't know what to think. Now that it was really happening, he didn't want me to come over. I demanded to know what was really going on. I was already afraid and suspicious. He said, "We need to talk."

CHAPTER **11**

Finding out the Truth

THE THINGS THAT I had been thinking were finally confirmed. He told me he hadn't shown up in Ireland because he wasn't the man in the picture. "Gabriel" was a fake name that he created for the online profile. Everything about Gabriel was a lie. He told me he wasn't a white man, he was black. He described himself to me as "black like a monkey in the jungle." He was only thirty-five, not fifty-three. He said I wouldn't like him because of his color. Then he continued telling me all the details, and how he ended up doing this. As I listened to him talking, I was speechless...I was so shocked. I was hurt and shaking. Suddenly, tears started rolling down my face. I sobbed so hard. I was not hurt because of the money—I was hurt because of the way I felt for Gabriel. I had feelings for him even though I'd never seen him, and now I realized I would never have any chance to know him at all.

My feelings for him made me want to stand by him no matter what. That was why I acted as I did, not knowing that it was only a trap. I was hurt because of the betrayal and the lies. How could I be so stupid? It was like the whole world had run me over. The whole time, I was sobbing. He finally asked me if I could find it in my heart to forgive him, while he continued, telling me that he was not Irish, and had never been to Ireland. He said he was originally from Nigeria. He want to make it sure that I will know this so he continue telling me that unfortunately Nigeria is the SCAMMER capital of the world. They probably originated from this country but I know for the fact that they are all over the world. Scammers are everywhere . These kind of people swarmed all over the internet like vultures looking for prey. I prayed while I was crying, and asked the Lord why this had happened to me. I still couldn't believe what I was hearing. I refused to accept the reality of the situation. I became deeply suspicious when he didn't show up in Ireland, but still I had given him the benefit of the doubt. As I was trying to calm down, I asked him why he had an Irish accent. He said he used to live in the UK for a while before he fled to Kenya, and that was how he got his accent.

He hurt my feelings so deeply. I had been waiting so patiently, and I had fallen in love with a picture. He told me that he was not really a scammer...he used to have a business, but he lost everything. As tears come rolling down my face. I ask him what kind of business he used to have. He told me that he got a store selling music equipment. He also wanted to have a music studio for people to record their songs. He said before his business fail. He use to own cars and he own his own house. But when the market crashed, his business crashed with it. He said he was too ashamed to go back to his family because of the disappointment. And

that he is an entrepreneur. That he can do lots
of things to make money. His friends wouldn't
help him when he asked for help. He realized
that he had no true friends. Now that he was
broke, everybody disappeared from his life.
They only wanted to be his friends when he
had money. The man continued with his story,
telling me he had a business degree—if I went
ahead with my trip, he said, he would show me
his diploma. He said he would make it up to
me. I asked him how he could do that—by paying me back? How could he do that, if he didn't
have a job? "Gabriel" said he would make sure
I had a good time when I was in Kenya, if I decided to come. He said that if I didn't want him
around while I was there, he would give me
one of his cell phones so that if I needed something or I encountered any kind of trouble, I
would call him and he would come over. He
said he understood why I didn't want him to be
around me, and he asked me again and again
to forgive him.

"Gabriel" told me that when he got to
Kenya from the UK, he had no friends, no

money, and nowhere to go. Then one day he talked to a couple of guys about jobs, and said he was looking for work. One guy told him that if he got a computer, they would give him something to do and he could make a lot of money. So the leader of the group gave him a lot of pictures and told him to put them on his hard drive so whenever he needed a picture, he'd already have it. He told "Gabriel" to create an on line profile based on the picture and to post it on any free dating site, since he had no money to pay for membership. "Gabriel" said he tried to ask where all the pictures came from, but he was told that all he needed to know was that he was from Europe, and he was a journalist. The group taught him everything he needed to know. They taught him how to talk like a woman if he was dealing with a man. He quickly became an expert and a very good liar. They taught him how to receive money if anyone ended up being willing to send it to him. He said it took him three weeks to create a good story. Then one day while he was browsing, he saw my profile. He knew I was new on that site, and immediately sent me an e-mail even though we were both standard members. He said he knew he had to find a way to pay for membership if I wouldn't do it, so he could communicate with me.

"Gabriel" said I was his first real victim. He knew just by talking to me that I was a good woman and an easy target. I asked him how he could do this to me—where was his conscience, or did he not even have one? He said he didn't have a choice. His friends in the UK wouldn't help him. No one would help him, and that was why he ended up in Kenya. While I was talking to him, I suggested that he probably had a better chance of getting a job in the UK, but he said he couldn't stay there...everything in the UK was monitored, just like in the United States, and he couldn't stay there any longer. I asked what he meant, and he said that he could stay in Kenya as long as he wanted without proper documentation. He kept telling me more about himself and why he fled to Kenya. Again, now that I knew who he was, I wasn't sure whether he was telling me the truth, since he'd already told me so many lies. I was thinking this might be another stunt to make me feel sorry for him. I told him that he was still young; he should repent and change his life before it was too late, so he wouldn't always have to watch his back and fear exposure. I told him it would be better to have freedom wherever he went, and that he should trust in God and pray for something good, rather than having to live in fear of being caught by the cops. I asked him what his real name was, but he wouldn't tell me. I told him he should use his amazing singing talent, or write a song, because he had a beautiful voice. He told me that he owned and sold music equipment; that was one of his businesses, and he loved music more than anything. So I encouraged him to pursue that dream. I told him that there was hope, and nothing was impossible as long as we trust God and do the right thing. I reminded him that life is a gift, and it is very short—why waste it?

After we had been talking for a while, he said that he had fallen in love with me. He said he could have gotten more money from me, but instead he choose to tell me the truth. He said he couldn't keep lying to me for money, that he couldn't bear not telling me the truth when he found out I was really coming to Kenya just to see whether he was really sick. He said it took a lot of courage and love for a woman to do such a thing, and that he was touched by my willingness to make a sacrifice for him. He said that I have lots of good qualities for a good woman, but the best quality is that I am a Christian and I have faith and I believe in God. He said he too use to go to church all the time. His parents raise him in the church. So why is he doing this evil act if he was raised in the church? No choice... He said. My faith was what made him feel the most guilty. While he was telling me all about himself, I asked him if he would use my picture on the internet, just like he used Gabriel's picture. He told me that he wouldn't do that because I am an older lady, and also he'd already deleted most of my pictures. He said most men wanted a younger woman, but of course I don't know if he was telling me the truth. I pray that he won't do anything with my picture. If he does, God will know it isn't me.

CHAPTER 12

Forgiveness

ALTHOUGH HE FINALLY told me the truth, he is still a liar. To this day, I cannot forget what happened As I acknowledge the trauma I've been through, I've decided to let go of my pain and hand the circumstances to God. I cannot do anything, but God can. I told "Gabriel" that all I could do is to forgive him. Forgiving is the right thing to do, regardless of how I feel. The devil is real, so I must do what I need to do. I told "Gabriel" that I wanted to move forward and I couldn't have hate in my heart. I told him I was not doing this for him; I was doing it for me. I can't keep dwelling on what happened. Not only was he too far away, this also happened outside the United States, and I don't think any authority can track him down, unless more people come forward to say that they were also victimized by the scam. "Gabriel" cannot pay me back, because he doesn't have a job. I felt a lot better after I told him that I forgave him.

He did thank me for forgiving him. He said that he wanted to go back home where his parents are. I felt a lot of doubt, so this time I wanted him to show me his face. At first he wouldn't, because he was afraid that I would tell the US cops about him. He was afraid that they would go after him in Kenya and put him in jail. I did not tell him that I had already talked to the police in Ireland and gave them all the information he had sent to me. I was still waiting for the results of that investigation. I couldn't tell him that I had reported him to the Irish authorities, because if I did, he might not show me his face. Instead, I said to him that there wasn't any reason for me to tell the cops, because this had happened overseas. It would be hard for the police to track him down, but if he kept doing this, sooner or later he would be caught.

This time, he agreed to show me his face on Skype. He said his name is Sean. When I heard the name, I had to asked why it doesn't sound Nigerian? He replied to me saying, his parents got that name from the British origin. Most young generations in Nigeria their names are somewhat English. While he was talking, I told him to stand up and turn around because I wanted to be sure that I was seeing a real person... and he did. When I saw his face, I started crying again. I had goosebumps, and I was shaking. I couldn't help it. I had been hoping it was just a bad dream, but now I knew for sure that the man in the picture, the one I'd learned to love, was not the man I had been talking to. Reality hurt so bad. Now I knew for sure that he didn't exist...I needed to forget the whole thing and move on.

For weeks, I had a hard time sleeping. I lost a lot of weight. My heart was broken. During this man's confession, I cried, because I was hurt. Even if the man told me he was sorry for what he did to me...then I asked him, who was Michael, the agent? I wanted to know everything, since he had started confessing. He told me that Michael was not really his agent; he was a banker in Kenya who received all of the con money. He told me that he didn't get 100% of the money he scammed online. He got only a portion of it, since he shared it with the banker and the person who gave him the pictures. So it was all a conspiracy. I told the man that he did all the work, but he didn't get all the profit. After knowing everything, it was hard to believe that this was happening to me. I had joined an international dating site hoping to find someone to share my life and who wanted companionship. I was expecting that I would find a husband the same way I found my first husband.

I can still remember how I met my husband. Back then, there were no computers, so we wrote to each other for two years before I decided to come out from my country, the Philippines, to the US to get married. When it came to money, my boyfriend, who then became my husband, was the one sending money to me so I could use it for all the documents I needed to get here, including my passport and my plane ticket. I never asked for money. I was too embarrassed to ask.

I came from a very poor family. In my younger years we barely have anything when it comes to so many things including food . If we have food, many times my grandpa divide it. We cannot have more since we only have very little. I always say I am still hungry. If I say that , he will tell me you can have it now but you won't eat later. It's your choice. I choose not to eat more. Sometimes we don't eat at all but we managed to survive and stay focused and think positively that once and for all blessing will come. Our life situation does not bother us that much because we have love, caring and understanding and stay together as a family. One of the great experience I have is when I go with our priest to visit and sing to poor people who lives in those remote areas in my country and bring them small gifts around Christmas time. Before, all my life I'd thought we are the poorest. Not until I start going out with our priest. Those family don't have no real house. They lived in a box without floors. The dirt is their floors. But I can see that the mother is trying to assist her children (there was two) in a way with respect and love. Then she start having tears when we handed her those gifts and sing to them Christmas songs. She was very thankful of what we did. That made my day when I saw that lady and her children smile. What I saw made me grateful of what my grandfather did for us. To this day I know I am blessed. Even though we are struggling we were teach good manners and respect of how to treat people the way we should be treated. One Sunday morning I decide to climbed on a tree to pick some fruit before I get ready for church. My grandfather did not like the idea which I did not let him know because I know that he won't allow me. It was very important for us to go to church first before we will do something else. It was too late when found out. I was already on top of the tree. This particular tree is high and big. So he came to where I was at with a big stick in his hand and told me to come down. I know my grandfather won't hesitate to use that stick to spank me once I am in the ground. I did disobey the rule by climbing the tree before we go to church. I knew he also fear that I might fall. I was a little stubborn when I was growing up. As soon as I saw that big old stick in his hand, I told him I am not coming down unless he will get rid of the stick. As if I can see my grandfather laughing as he turned around and left with the stick so then I came down and get ready for church. That was the good old days. That is how I was brought up. We don't have the material things that most people have. Our grandfather teaches us to be content and appreciate of what we have no matter what. He keep on saying that it still a blessing even if it's only a little. This is one reason why I get embarrassed to ask especially when it comes to money. So when my boyfriend who became my husband send me money I don't take it for granted. I spent the money wisely but I don't ask for more. He willingly and patiently sent it to me for a certain period of time until I was ready to come over. I do not want to take advantage of his goodness and generosity towards me. I know he loves me because he was not asking anything in return in spite the fact that it took me that long (two years) to make the decision to come over to be with him. He was not selfish, he understands nor he doesn't demand anything .

He patiently waited for me. That is real love. That kind of LOVE been long gone. In some occasions we run out of things to say in our letters since we wrote each other constantly. So we sent unusual things on top of those love letters like dried leaves, rocks, sometimes dried flowers. From different countries, since he travels for his job being in the U.S. Navy. He sent me all kinds of things not only money just to let me know that he loves me and he is thinking about me. In fact, I used some of the money to call him long distance so I could hear his voice. This was the only thing he didn't know—that I used some of the money to call him. Back then it was a lot harder, because there were no computers or cell phones. But we managed to write just about every day in order to get to know each other, and we sent lots of pictures by mail so we would know what the other looked like. He express his love through his letters by writing almost everyday. So I did the same in return by answering his letters daily. We cannot tell who receive the most. All we know is we express the way we care to each other through those words by writing letters. This was the sacrifice we did for two years. The first time when I arrived in this country which was in Hawaii in the island of Oahu, where he got stationed, after doing his tour of Sea duty . He took me to this apartment that he rented for us to stay. First thing that he showed me when I got inside, was those love letters that I wrote for him. It amazed me upon knowing that he saves all that to show it to me how much he cares about me. It was full of a big Sea bag of love letters. We barely know each other as we sat down and start having a conversation and get acquainted to each other, I immediately mentioned to Terry (this is what his name) to send me back to the country to which I came from if he won't marry me. I did not tell him that as soon as I step up to get into the plane I suddenly felt homesick. I wanted to go back home. I was having a cold feet. Terry understood that we don't have time to waste. My visa will only allow me to stay here in U.S. for three months. In a worse case scenario if he won't marry me within that time frame the immigration will send me back to the Philippines. As soon as Terry heard me telling him about my concern he hugged me and tell me not to worry. He said that this is the moment he'd been waiting for. He told me how much he loved me and wanted me to be his wife. Then he showed me a ring which he already purchased before I arrived and put it into my ring finger to prove to me that he didn't change his mind. I was electrified by the way I felt at that moment then I start crying with joy. This person had been waiting for me for a long time. I don't need to leave. He does love me... Before the ninety day was over we became husband and wife. That is what you call real love. You cannot find this kind of love anymore. Men nowadays are more reserve and selfish and kind of just more into playing games. They don't know what they want. In other words they are unstable when it comes to many different ways. In those days, people were more honest and serious. Things change, and people change drastically. Now it's even harder to find the right person because of so many dishonest individual everywhere .But this was why I joined the international site—I was willing to make the sacrifice once again, if I met the right person.

All of us are dealing with different issues in our lives. Mine was unique, but I never let it destroy my life. People at work did not know that I was undergoing such painful circumstances. They didn't know what was going on— not even my friends knew. I went to work as if nothing had happened. The only thing anyone noticed was that I lost a lot of weight. I went from 120 pounds to 110 pounds. All I did most of the time was keep praying to the Lord our God to give me strength.

This time, "Gabriel" told me that deep in his heart, he appreciated me and thanked me for forgiving him. But I had a hard time believing him. He said that if I didn't come to Kenya, we would never be able to meet. This was the last chance. After his confession, I didn't really care. I was not interested, and he was no longer part of my plan now that I knew who he was. He didn't know that I had already changed all my plans. I didn't tell him that I already cancelled my hotel reservation and my flight. I lost quite a bit of money because of the cancellations, and I'd had to pay out of pocket for the vaccines. But I had to do what was necessary; otherwise I would be forced to go even though I did not want to see this person. I was so hurt—I didn't ever want to talk to him again. But he still wanted me to fall in love with him.

He kept telling me to let him know what I wanted him to do to make up for all the pain he caused me. He told me that he was not bad-looking; he was tall and slim, but he was black. He kept reminding me that the reason he didn't use his real picture was because of his color. I told him I'm not judgmental; my skin is brown, because I am originally from the Philippines. I told him that the most important thing is the heart of a person—what he is like inside. I also told him that he was too young for me, and I was looking for an older man closer to my age. Then he quoted, and said, "If my presence won't change anything, then my absence won't make any difference." Then he told me his real name and I said there was a favor he could do for me. I wanted him to find out who the man really was in the picture he'd been using. I remembered he told me that the first time he met with the group, before they gave him Gabriel's picture, he said he overheard them saying that he was a journalist and he lived somewhere in Europe—one of the team of scammers knew where he was from. The information about being from Ireland was created for the profile.

The man I was talking to said he didn't know where Gabriel was from, and his only goal was to use his picture. One person in the group, the mastermind, knew everything about the real Gabriel; that was why he had so many of his photos. I asked if Gabriel knew that his photos had been used on the online dating sites as well as on Facebook. I wondered whether Gabriel was really the mastermind behind all this—that he allowed them to use his picture to get money and scam people because of his good looks.

CHAPTER 13

Getting the Information About the Picture

I KNOW NOWADAYS anyone can get pictures and information on a person. But because I couldn't believe that he would just let all his information be out in the open for people to see, I decided to tell the con man to find out and get if for me so I could at least let the real Gabriel know what was going on. But I didn't tell him that was my plan. I also reminded him that if he really cared about me, he would find out the information for me. He said that once he did that, he'd be out of the picture. I really wondered what this man wanted...did he

want me to love him, as I had loved Gabriel?
Who knew what he was really up to this time.

One day he finally agreed, and said that he
would get the information about Gabriel, but
it would be risky. He said it was risky because
when the group gave him the picture, he separated from them and got his own place, which
was four or five hours away from these people.
Afterward, he created the profile for Gabriel's
picture on his own. He didn't want to be in the
same house with the group. He said he wanted
to be alone and have his own place, so he could
have privacy. In order for him to get the information, he would have to go back to where he
started and get reacquainted with the group,
and pretend that he would join them again. He
told me that he needed a whole week to do it.
He left his city, Lavington, that Monday to go
to Mombasa Road and told me that he should
have all of Gabriel's information by the following Sunday morning.

The day he arrived in that place, he told
me that we couldn't talk for very long on the
phone because he didn't want them to know

what he was talking about. He said he could talk to me on Yahoo! Messenger, but not all the time, since there were five of them (all men) living in a small three-bedroom house. He was number six. He said that it was not going to be easy for him to do the task, but he would do as he promised. It was very crowded in that house; most of the time he slept in the living room. During his stay with these men, he said it was an ordeal for him. Every single day, if they were not on the computer, they watched sports on TV, drank, and smoked pot, and had women over regularly. He said that he told lies for money, which he knew was wrong, but he wouldn't do what these people had been doing all the time; it was just too rowdy for him. He said that he could hardly wait to get back to Lavington where he had his own quiet place, but he couldn't just steal the information from the group mastermind, because it was in his computer, and he didn't want the mastermind to know why he was there. He said he was on friendly terms with the youngest person there, who was close to him and would get the information from him, since he had access to the leader's computer. He said he would make this sacrifice to give me what I wanted. So I just waited to see what would happen next. I talked to him once on the phone, and he said he could talk only briefly—the group was there listening. He said that he would be ready to go home as soon as he got the information, and that he would text me as he promised, with Gabriel's information.

Within a matter of days, as I was waiting for him, my phone finally rang. I knew who it was—it was a text message from the man. This was the moment I had been waiting for. I can't describe the way I felt at that moment. Why should I do this to a man who doesn't even know who I am? Why should I care? But my gut was telling me to do it. I felt anxious to know the information. After all this time, I would have the chance to find out Gabriel's real name, where he lived, his phone number and real e-mail address. The moment finally came. To my surprise, I found out that Gabriel was not from Ireland. He was not a journalist, as the mastermind had said. He was from eastern Europe and owned a bookstore. The con-artist told me that he didn't know that they have a person from the country of Latvia. He continued telling me all he knows is they have few men that lives here in the U.S , few are from Ireland, some are in India but most of them are in UK. I wondered if these are men and women who are members of the group or maybe these are people that their identity had been stolen and this scammers got their information saved in the database of their computer .Then they use their information and posted it in the Internet to gain money. I still remember how the leader of the group got Gabriel's pictures and he said he might willingly sent it to them. I don't know exactly what he meant by this. I was thinking could it be the same way of what I did since I sent this con-artist some of my pictures because I didn't know the truth who he was in the first place. Could it be that Gabriel was on the online dating as well. Who knows.... I told the man now that I had what I needed, this would probably be the end of our communication. I could tell that he wanted us to continue talking. He told me again how he felt toward me. I contradicted him and said he didn't know what love is—that he was self-centered and loved only himself, that he had victimized people for his own benefit. I did not hesitate to let him know that I felt nothing for him—if I had feelings, they would be for Gabriel. He told me that there was no Gabriel; he had been talking to me all this time, so he was the one I had feelings for. He wanted me to fell the same towards him as how I felt for Gabriel. This man is insane. He expect me to fall in love with him after finding out this horrible truth of what he did to me. Again he tried to persuade me as if he done nothing wrong. He must be out of his mind. I reminded him that I hadn't known who he really was—that if he had told me and shown me his face, I wouldn't have gone on talking to him.

I told him I couldn't trust him, because with all the lies he had told, he would surely lie again. His entire life was a lie, and he had been doing it for so long that by this time he probably couldn't tell the difference between a lie and the truth. He said he would change, but first he wanted to go home to Nigeria as soon as he had enough money for his plane ticket. As soon as he said this, I wanted to let him know that he had lost the credibility I needed to believe and trust him. He said that he had contacted an old friend back home who was willing to help him out. Even though I was still hurt, I said that was great. At that time, I didn't really care what he did with his life.

CHAPTER 14

Communicating with the Man in the Picture

WHEN I HAD Gabriel's information, the very next day I called his phone. I wasn't sure if it was a cell phone or a home phone—someone answered and then hung up. The third time I called, he finally stayed on the line and I introduced myself. He said something, but I couldn't understand what he was saying. I was thinking maybe it would be better to e-mail him so I could explain and introduce myself. In my e-mail, I told him who I was and how I ended up with his information. My e-mail was not long. After a couple of days, I hadn't heard from him, so I e-mailed again telling him why I was contacting him. I thought he might not answer because he didn't know who I was, or maybe he was just confused about the whole thing. A day or two after the second message, Gabriel wrote back to me. He said that he answered the phone when I called, but he couldn't understand what I was saying, and he was also having a hard time understanding my e-mail. He was very confused, and all of this had come out of nowhere. He told me in one of his emails that he tried to answer but I hang up. He didn't speak English well, but he said he had lots of questions for me. He asked how I got his contact information. Apparently some people from Kenya contacted him also through email. The person mentioned that he is a cop in Kenya and he had some kind of information about who the scammers are. But he didn't answer because he didn't know who he is. He'd ask me if I knew the person. I wrote back and told him that a cop from Kenya also contacted me through email. I told him I don't how those cops from Kenya got my email address maybe the scammers give it to them. Gabriel don't understand. So I have to explained everything as well as I could, and told him the purpose of contacting him was to say that he was the victim of identity theft—someone stole his information and used it on the internet, mostly for online dating. The people who stole his identity had also created a profile on Facebook with Gabriel's name. They used the same photos on Facebook that they had used for online dating.

At first he said that he didn't really believe me, since in the past he also received more e-mail from someone but he had not answered because he did not know the person, and that person didn't say much in their message. He told me that he would never do bad things to people for money. He owned a bookstore in Riga, Latvia and he was very happy. He didn't understand much about computers, so he rarely used one. Mainly he used the computer to communicate with the bank for his business.

Gabriel told me that if I could get the scammers arrested, he would come to the United States to watch the verdict. He didn't understand that it was hard for me to have them prosecuted since it was an international issue. He tried to ask and answer questions, even though his English wasn't good. He said he used Google to translate everything. His English translation was somewhat broken, but he did try to ask and answer as many questions as he could. I told him how I got involved in his life, and I told him that I understood if he didn't really believe me. He said that he appreciated everything I had done.

I invited him to join Facebook under his real identity, but he said that in eastern Europe they don't use Facebook, instead they use V.K.com, which is similar. He wanted me to go on that site and invite him as a friend so we could communicate more. I decided not to join; instead I asked him to send me some pictures with his bookstore in the background. He did e-mail me back with pictures taken of himself at work. He looked much older than in the photos used by the con artist, but he was still a handsome man. The people who stole his identity must have had his pictures for a while, since he looked so much younger in the photos they had used. They must have used his photos repeatedly online and on various websites because of his good looks.

During this time, the Irish authorities finally contacted me. They informed me of the results of their investigation into who Gabriel really was. They found out that he did book a flight to arrive on the 10th of September (that was the day I went to pick him up at the airport) but never actually paid for the flight. He got a reservation reference number to give me, to make it look as if he had booked a flight. From other inquiries carried out, they had no record of him. They told me their conclusion was that unfortunately, I was the victim of a scam by an unknown individual. They told me that the passport I showed them was a fake. The police told me they were very sorry that this experience affected my stay in Ireland. They suggested that I should report the matter to the authorities for further investigation here in the US, and that is exactly what I did, but the police couldn't do anything about it because it happened outside the country. They said that if I had more issues that needed their help, I should e-mail them, and they would do the best they could. I sent a reply to the police in Ireland telling them what I knew, and I told them they were right, and that the person who victimized me had confessed. I thanked them for their efforts to help me.

The last time I heard from the man who victimized me was a month ago. He told me that he was back in his country, and that he was going back to church. He said that he would try his best to start over and do the right thing, and follow my advice to pursue a singing career.

This is my true story. If I can prevent one person from being victimized by a scam through my story that means I am doing great....and I'm glad to have my story published ..

Remy Hetrick

Summary

IN THIS BOOK, the author tells the story of how she was victimized by an online dating scam. An unknown individual pretended to be a good-looking man, whom she met through an international dating site. She describes how he persuaded her and made her believe that he was for real. She describes the lies that led her to realize she was the victim of a scam... but then, in an unexpected turn of events, the man lying to her confesses his true identity, because he has fallen in love with her and hopes to continue a relationship. Remy describes how she finds out the true identity of the man whose pictures she saw online, and how she finds forgiveness and closure despite her heartbreak.